WANTED

A FEW BOLD RIDERS

ODYSSEY

In memory of Charles Tyler Hill
August 3, 1990 - January 13, 1996

Like Pony Express Riders, Tyler was young and brave.
He contended with a malignant tumor rather than bandits or mountains.
And yet, he would grin from beneath his favorite Batman hat and flash
"I love you" in American Sign Language with the fingers of his right hand.
He rides on in our hearts. — D.B.

To my wife Carol and children CaryAnn and Tom.
May you always be adventurous. — T.A.

Copyright © 1997 Trudy Corporation, 353 Main Avenue, Norwalk, CT 06851,
and the Smithsonian Institution, Washington, DC, 20560.

Soundprints is a division of Trudy Corporation, Norwalk, Connecticut.

Book Design: Shields & Partners, Westport, CT

First Edition 1997
10 9 8 7 6 5 4 3 2 1
Printed in Hong Kong

Library of Congress Cataloging-in-Publication Data

Bailer, Darice.

Wanted — a few bold riders : a story of the Pony Express /
by Darice Bailer : illustrated by Tom Antonishak.
      p.   cm.
Summary: While visiting the Pony Express exhibit at the National Postal Museum, Kevin travels
back in time and becomes Warren Upson, a famous rider with a difficult route.
      ISBN 1-56899-464-8 (hardcover) ISBN 1-56899-465-6 (pbk.)
1. Pony express — Juvenile Fiction. [1. Pony express — Fiction. 2. Upson, Warren — Fiction.
3. Time travel — Fiction. 4. Postal Service — Fiction.
5. National Postal Museum (United States) —Fiction.] I. Antonishak, Tom, ill. II. Title.
      P27.B1447Wan 1997   97-7206
      [E] — dc21   CIP
                                          AC

WANTED
A FEW BOLD RIDERS

Written by Darice Bailer
Illustrated by Tom Antonishak

Soundprints
Where Children Discover...

"Tomas, be careful with those buttons!" Lucy pleads. "If you break anything in the exhibit, we'll be in big trouble. They'll never let us visit this museum again."

Tomas, Lucy, and their friends Kevin and Emma, are at the National Postal Museum of the Smithsonian Institution in Washington, D.C. Tomas is hitting some orange buttons on a display case in the exhibit on the Pony Express. When Tomas presses one of the buttons, a question appears on a screen.

Emma is reading information printed on storyboards about the brave young men who carried mail, newspapers and important news by pony, back and forth along the Overland Trading Route, from St. Joseph, Missouri to Sacramento, California from 1860–1861. Kevin is looking at a map on the wall that shows the entire route.

"It took ten days to deliver the mail to San Francisco?" Emma asks.

"I could have delivered the mail a whole lot faster!" exclaims Tomas.

"You have to remember, Tomas," Lucy says, "that airplanes and mail trucks hadn't been invented yet. Neither had televisions, computers, or radios. I'd like to see you *try* to deliver the mail on a pony in less than ten days!"

"Look at this!" shouts Emma.

She is standing in front of a log cabin. A video is playing on a large screen inside the doorway. A man wearing a fringed, buckskin jacket is talking. "I signed up," the man is saying. "I was on the first Pony Express run."

Kevin, Lucy, and Tomas rush over to catch what the man is saying. He says his name is Warren Upson but that people called him by his nickname, Boston.

"I ended up dragging that pony behind me more than I sat on top of it," the man says. He tells how he pulled his pony through flooded streams and over snow-capped mountains. Then Boston places his hat back on his head. "Gotta ride, partners!" he says. Kevin turns away from the screen, then gasps at what he sees.

"**R**eady to leave Friday's Station, Boston?" Kevin hears a man say. "It's time to saddle up and head out."

The man is leading a mustang pony toward Kevin. In the distance, he sees mountains. He hears the mustang whinny.

Wow, Kevin exclaims to himself as he strokes the pony. *This man thinks I'm Boston Upson.*

A rider gallops toward him, dust clouding the path behind him. The man pulls in the reins and leaps off his pony. The stationmaster lifts off the rider's *mochila* from the saddle bag on his pony and heaves it onto the mustang he's preparing for Kevin.

That mochila is what they carry the mail in, Kevin thinks.

"Trail's clear, Jack," the rider says to the stationmaster.

"No robbers or horse thieves tonight, Pony Bob?" the stationmaster asks.

"Not a one," replies Pony Bob. "They wouldn't dare hold up the Pony Express."

"Those gun-toting bandits learned their lesson on that last ride," Jack says. "Bob was brave, wasn't he, Boston?"

Kevin nods eagerly. He can't wait to find out what happened to Bob.

"I didn't see those bandits until I came around a curve on the trail," Bob says. "And there they were — two bandits, with bandannas tied around their faces. They were sitting on their ponies just waiting for me, guns pointing straight at my chest. 'Throw up your hands, or you're a dead man!' they said. 'Give us your pony and the mail!' "

Jack whistles while Bob takes a deep breath.

"I told them, 'You'll have to catch me first,' " Bob continues. "And before they could even fire a shot, my pony and I were gone."

"I shouldn't be wasting time talking," Bob says, then turns to Kevin. "South Carolina soldiers fired their guns at Fort Sumter. There's a war on!"

Bob must mean the Civil War, Kevin thinks. *On April 12, 1861, war broke out in the United States between the North and South.*

Pony Bob pats the mochila. "There's an article from a South Carolina newspaper inside telling what happened. Boston, you've got to make good time on this run. Since your father is the editor of the Sacramento *Union* newspaper, he'll want this news right away."

"So the war between the states has finally begun," Jack exclaims, shaking his head. "It's up to you now, Boston, to bring Californians this sad news."

"Hurry, Boston," Pony Bob urges. "And don't let the snow bury you in those mountains. You don't want telegraph wires to reach California before you do."

"Right, Bob," Kevin replies. He puts his left foot in the stirrup and swings his right foot over the pony's back. Then he digs in his heels.

"Whoa, Boston," Jack shouts, calling him back. "I have to record your departure time." Jack scratches the time on the time log with a quill pen. Then he tucks the time sheet into one of the brown leather pockets on the mochila and locks it.

"Nice job," Jack says to Pony Bob. "You're one hour early on your usual four-hour run. That ought to help Boston if he finds trouble in those mountains. Do you think you can keep up a fast pace?" Jack asks, turning to Kevin.

"If Bob completed his route ahead of schedule," Kevin replies, "I can do the same!"

"That's not so easy, Boston," Jack says, "considering your route is about sixty miles. I'm forgetting how fast you and the other riders rode to deliver President Lincoln's inaugural speech in seven days and seventeen hours."

"And I aim to help beat that now," Kevin says, cocking his hat. "Godspeed!" Pony Bob and Jack both shout as Kevin and his pony gallop off, kicking up a cloud of dust.

"I'm riding a pony!" Kevin shouts. He wishes his friends could see him now.

Kevin's eyes open wide when his pony neighs at what looks to be a pack of dogs. Kevin looks closely and sees that the animals aren't dogs. They're a pack of wolves, and they're howling. They look hungry and mean.

Kevin's heart pounds wildly as the wolves close in on him. The wolves snarl and bare their teeth.

"Let's get out of here!" Kevin yells. He snaps the reins and spurs the pony on with his heels. The pony gallops down the trail, just ahead of the wolves.

When they have outdistanced the wolves, Kevin lets the pony slow down. "Good boy," Kevin says, patting his pony. "Thank goodness you're fast. Those wolves looked pretty hungry to me."

17

    As they ride farther up into the mountains,
Kevin and his pony face another danger — snow.
    A gusty wind begins to whip the snow around as they ride. Icy
flakes sting Kevin's face and hands. Snowdrifts pile higher than
the pony. Kevin shivers from the cold.
    The pony steps confidently along the trail, as if it has traveled
this route many times. "It's a good thing you know the way,"
Kevin says. "The trail markings are hidden under all this snow."
    At times, the snow is so deep that Kevin hops off his pony. He
swishes through the snow, cutting a path with his legs, pulling his

pony behind him. Kevin knows he has to be careful where he steps. The cliff near the trail hovers over a deep canyon. One wrong step and Kevin and his pony could end up in the gorge hundreds of feet below.

Kevin is cold and hungry. But he knows he cannot quit. "If you're a Pony Express rider, you have to follow the oath," Kevin says, talking out loud to break the loneliness. "No swearing. No drinking. And you promise to think about the mail first, your pony second, and yourself third."

"The mail must go through. The mail must go through," Kevin repeats to himself, trudging on. "If I don't reach the next station, how will people find out about Fort Sumter? How will they ever know that the Civil War has begun?"

Finally, Kevin and his pony reach the other side of the mountain. As they begin descending toward the valley, the snow turns to heavy rain. Kevin is soaked.

"Delivering this mail isn't easy," Kevin says to his pony. "No wonder the Pony Express used the best ponies, like you!" *And the boldest riders, too,* Kevin thinks to himself as he charges into Yank's Station.

The stationmaster hands Kevin a mug of coffee. He grabs it and guzzles it down. It quiets his chattering teeth and warms his icy hands. As soon as he finishes the last drop, Kevin hops on a fresh pony and gallops off.

When Kevin reaches the American River, the water rushes past him, spilling over the banks. Kevin looks around but does not see a bridge for him to cross. He has no choice but to wade across the swollen river with his pony.

Before he does, Kevin hops off his pony and removes the mochila. He holds it on his head, like a bonnet. As long as his elbows don't touch the water, he knows the mochila — and the mail — will stay dry.

Kevin leads the pony into the river. Suddenly the pony stumbles into a deep hole and its head plunges beneath the surface of the water. Kevin lifts the mochila high above his head, holding the reins tightly until his pony regains its footing and rises up in the water.

Kevin and his pony are soaked, but the mail is dry!

It's not much longer before Kevin arrives at Strawberry Station. The stationmaster has seen Boston approaching and already has a fresh pony ready for the next leg of the journey.

Kevin is exhausted and hungry. But he knows that Pony Express riders are only supposed to stop for two minutes at each station, so he tries his best to stay awake.

Quickly, Kevin tells the stationmaster the news he's delivering. The stationmaster shakes his head sadly when he hears that war has begun.

"The President is going to need help fighting to preserve the Union," the stationmaster says. "I think I had better turn this station over to my helper and join the Union troops."

If it hadn't been for the Pony Express, Kevin thinks, *it could have been weeks before this man heard about the war.*

Kevin gulps down some water from a tin cup, quickly eats a piece of cornbread, and dashes off once more. He hopes he can make it in record time. The sky is clear, the ground is dryer than it was in the mountains, and dirt is easier to travel through than snow and rivers.

Eleven miles later, at Webster's Station, Kevin changes ponies and picks up new mail. Twelve miles later, at Moss Station, he does the same. He is able to average eleven miles per hour as he heads to the next station, Sportsman's Hall.

Sportsman's Hall is Boston's last stop. Kevin is so tired that he practically falls off his pony. The stationmaster laughs. "Last time you fell asleep in your saddle. Well, I guess this is an improvement."

Exhausted, Kevin tries to keep his eyes open. The stationmaster turns to speak to a man walking out of the station. "Sam, it's time for you to take over. Get this mail to Sacramento."

"Trail's clear," Kevin says to Sam, repeating what Pony Bob said to him.

Sam lifts his hat in a salute to Kevin and the Sportsman's Hall stationmaster.

"Godspeed, Sam!" Kevin shouts, waving good bye. "You're carrying important news!"

The stationmaster pats Kevin on the back. "Now you go on inside and eat, Boston. You've got yourself two days to rest before Sam returns. Then you'll be heading back east. Who knows what news Sam will bring us."

The stationmaster leads Kevin's pony toward a stable along the wall. He hands him off to a young man for feeding and grooming.

"The Pony Express beats a stagecoach or steamship any day," the young man declares as he feeds Kevin's pony some oats.

"Through sleet or snow," Kevin says. *Delivering the mail may be different nowadays, but the weather is still the same!* he adds to himself.

Inside the cabin, Kevin takes some steaming oatmeal from a black pot resting above a fire. He is relieved finally to be able to take a rest.

ow Kevin understands why Pony Express riders like Boston Upson are honored in books and museums. Riders like Boston were usually 18 to 25 years old and very brave. They were often lonely and scared out on their trail. But they knew that many people depended on them. The Pony Express service was the fastest way to communicate across our nation's unsettled western land.

Kevin hears laughter. He looks around to find himself back in the museum, surrounded by his friends. Tomas is still hitting the orange buttons. "True or false?" Tomas asks. "Buffalo Bill was one of the most daring Pony Express riders."

"False," Kevin says.

"You're right," Tomas replies. "It says here that we aren't sure that Buffalo Bill actually rode the Pony Express. But how did you know that?"

Kevin smiles and points to the video. The man portraying Boston Upson is once again telling his story in the cabin doorway.

"It just had to be him," Kevin says. "Boston was the bravest of all."

ABOUT THE PONY EXPRESS

In 1860, half a million people lived in new settlements in California, Nevada, and Utah, in the western part of the United States. These pioneers didn't want to wait three weeks for mail to arrive by stagecoach or up to six months for the mail to arrive by ship. They demanded quicker mail and news, especially when a civil war threatened to divide the nation.

On April 3, 1860 the Pony Express mail service, founded by William Russell, Alexander Majors, and William Waddell, began to provide settlers with faster service. Brave young men, mostly between the ages of 18 and 25, carried mail, news and government documents on pony. They rode 1,966 miles from St. Joseph, Missouri to Sacramento, California with the mail locked in four *cantinas* or pockets on their Pony Express *mochila* or saddle cover. They delivered the mail in ten days, cutting the previous time — by stagecoach (three weeks) or ship (four weeks or more) — in half. They earned $25 a week.

Riders handed off the mail to one another in a relay chain. Each rider changed to a fresh pony every 10–12 miles at one of 190 stations spread across eight states and territories. He stopped no longer than two minutes at each station. The rider changed ponies as many as seven times during his run. The Pony Express used close to 500 mustang ponies because mustangs were, like the men who rode them, spirited, tough, and hardy.

Pony and rider formed a courageous team. They galloped through the woods and across the desert, rivers, and mountains, in rainstorms or blizzards, by day or night. They dodged buffalo herds, bandits, and wild animals. Despite heart-pounding danger, only one rider died and only one mochila of mail was lost.

Pony Express riders followed the Central Overland route that was used by stagecoaches, covered wagons, and pack mules during the United States' westward migration. The trail wound through states and territories that supported the Union in its opposition to slavery.

Riders obeyed the Pony Express rule to think of the mail first, their pony second, and themselves third. They swore an oath not to curse, drink, or fight.

On October 24, 1861, the transcontinental telegraph was completed, strung along the Central Overland route. Messages were transmitted across the country in a single day and at a cheaper price than the Pony Express.

Two days after telegraph operation began, the Pony Express mail service ended. It lasted just 18 months but proved that communication across the western wilderness was possible in all seasons. Riders crossed terrain once thought impassable. They ushered in both the transcontinental telegraph and railroad and stories of their courage captivated a nation for years to come.

GLOSSARY

American River: a river in California that runs down from the Sierra Nevada Mountains and empties into the Sacramento River in Sacramento.

cantina: hard leather pockets sewn onto the *mochila* to secure the mail and papers carried by the Pony Express. The *cantinas* were locked until the mail reached its final destination.

canyon: a deep river valley with steep mountain sides.

Civil War: fought in the United States from 1861–1865. The Union, or northern states, fought the Confederacy, or southern states. The Confederacy broke off and formed its own government for economic and political reasons.

Godspeed: a good-bye wish that a traveler be successful in his or her journey.

gorge: a deep valley with steep rocky sides.

mochila: (pronounced mo-CHEE-la) the leather saddle cover that fits over a pony's regular saddle. Pony Express riders rode on top of the *mochila*, which was used to carry mail and other documents in four hard, leather pockets called *cantinas*.

quill pen: a pen made from a bird's feather. The quill was carved to form a point and dipped in ink for writing.

Sierra Nevada Mountains: mountains in California and Nevada.

stagecoach: a four-wheeled carriage pulled by several horses. The coach carried mail, packages, and people over long distances, averaging only 4–5 miles per hour.

steamship: a ship powered by a steam engine.